AF316813

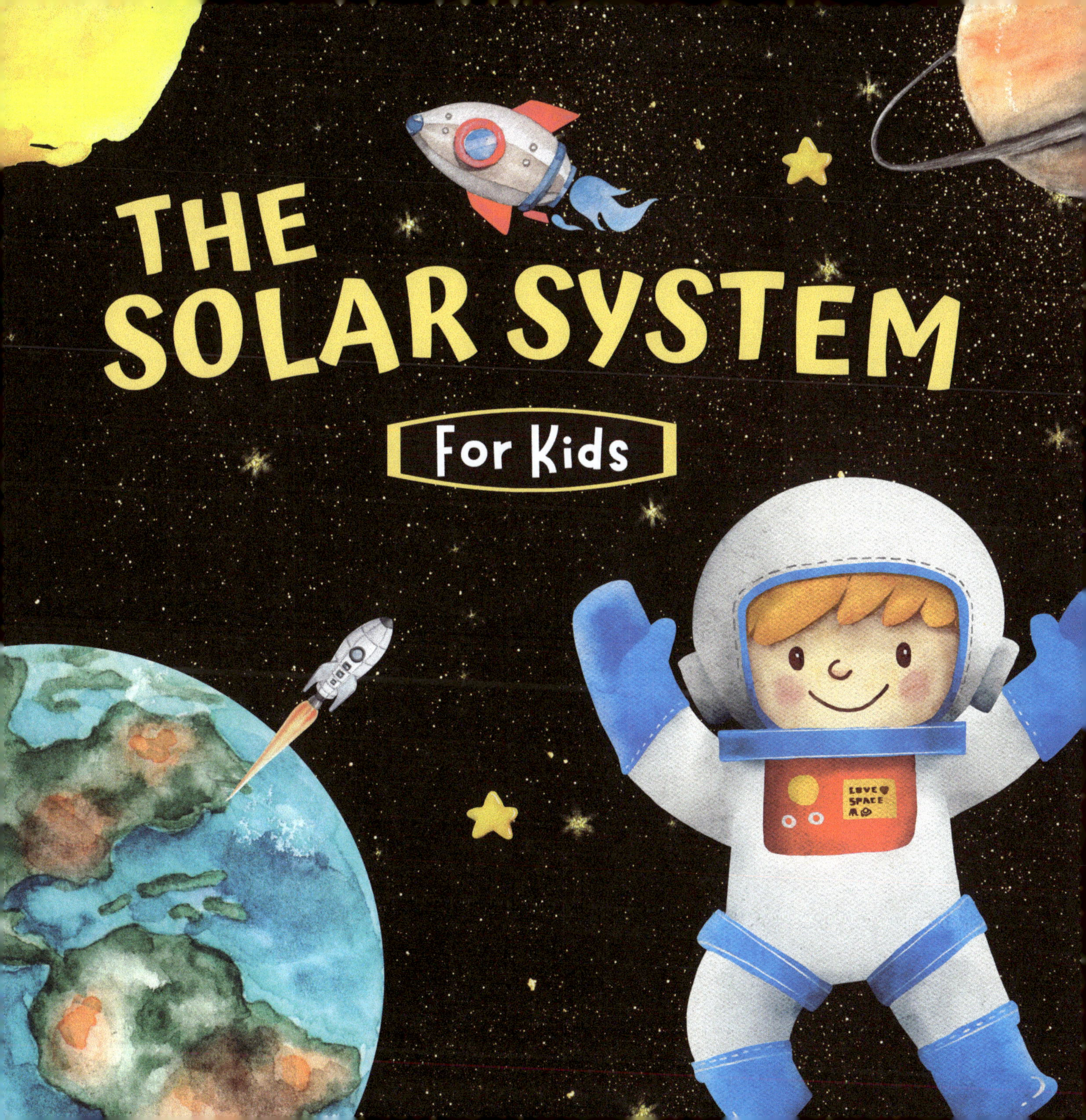

THE
SOLAR SYSTEM
For Kids

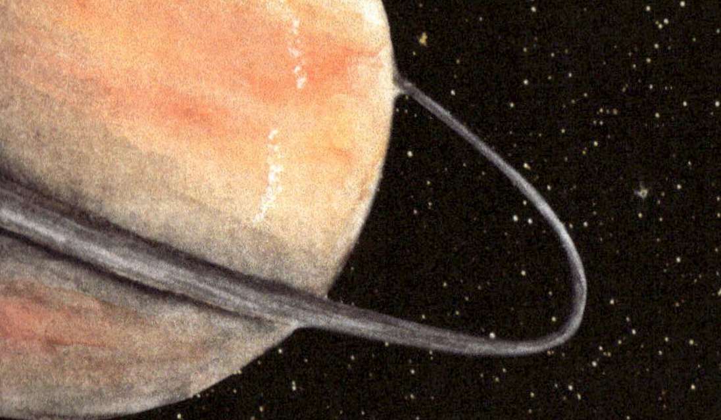

ISBN: 978-84-126776-9-0

 contacto@samueljohnbooks.com

 www.facebook.com/bookssamueljohn/

www.amazon.com/author/samueljohnbooks

LET'S GET STARTED!

MERCURY

Mercury is the smallest planet in our solar system. It is also the closest planet to the Sun.

VENUS

Venus is the second closest planet to the Sun.

EARTH

Earth is the planet we live on. It is the third from the Sun. Although it is called Earth, most of its surface is water.

MARS

Mars is known as "the Red Planet" due to its color.

JUPITER

Jupiter is the largest planet
in our solar system.

SATURN

Saturn is the second-largest planet in our solar system. It is not the only one with rings, but his are the most visible from our planet.

URANUS

Uranus was the first planet discovered with a telescope.

NEPTUNE

Neptune is the planet in our system that is farthest from the Sun.

THE SUN

The Sun is a star. It is located in the center of our solar system.

All the planets revolve around the Sun.

It takes the Earth one year to make a full revolution around the Sun. A total of 365 days.

THE MOON

The Moon is the satellite of the Earth. It revolves around our planet.

It has no light of its own. It shines due to the reflection of the sunlight.

And here it ends!
I hope you liked it and learned new things.
Until next time!

I want to ask you a favor so that this book reaches more people, and that is that you rate it with a sincere opinion on the platform where you purchased it.

With that small gesture, you will be helping me to carry on with new projects.

I can't wait to start creating my next book for you!

See you soon!

THE SOLAR SYSTEM
For Kids
Ages 3-6

VOLCANOES
For Kids

HUMAN BODY
Systems

THE MOST
FAMOUS
Landmarks
IN THE WORLD

FASCINATING
UNIVERSE
facts

THE
WATER CYCLE
For Kids

PREHISTORY
For Kids

ANCIENT
EGYPT

SCAN ME

www.ingramcontent.com/pod-product-compliance
Lightning Source LLC
Chambersburg PA
CBHW040736150726

48196CB00011B/625